Rocks and Stones

Rita Storey

W
FRANKLIN WATTS

00 400 876 821

Sch

First published in 2006 by
Franklin Watts
338 Euston Road
London NW1 3BH

Franklin Watts Australia
Hachette Children's Books
Level 17/207 Kent Street
Sydney NSW 2000

Copyright © Franklin Watts 2006

Art director: Jonathan Hair
Series designed and created for Franklin Watts by Painted Fish Ltd.
Designer: Rita Storey
Editor: Fiona Corbridge

Picture credits:
Corbis/Peter Beck p. 24, p. 18 (bottom); istockphoto.com p. 6, p. 7, p. 8, p. 9, p. 10, p. 11, p. 12, p. 13, p. 14, p. 15, p. 16, p. 17, p. 18 (top), p. 19 (top), p. 20, p. 21, p. 22, p. 23 (top), p. 25, p. 27 (top); Tudor Photography p. 18 (bottom), p. 19 (bottom), p. 26, p. 27 (bottom); www.holloways.co.uk p. 23 (bottom).

Cover images: Tudor Photography, Banbury; www.holloways.co.uk (bottom).

ISBN-10: 0 7496 6454 1
ISBN-13: 978 0 7496 6454 1
Dewey classification: 552

A CIP catalogue record for this book is available from the British Library.

Printed in China

Northamptonshire Libraries & Information Service	
00 400 876 821	
Peters	31-Aug-06
552	£11.99

Contents

What are rocks and stones? 6

Where do rocks come from? 8

Mining and quarrying 10

Building materials 12

Cement and concrete 14

Building with concrete 16

At home 18

In the street 20

In the garden 22

Rocks and stones in art 24

Gemstones 26

Glossary 28

Index 30

Words in **bold** are
in the glossary.

What are rocks and stones?

Rock is a **natural material** that is found above and below the ground. Stones are small pieces of rock.

There are rocky cliffs and mounds of rock above the ground. People like to climb them.

Large pieces of rock are called boulders and are very hard and heavy.

The wind, rain and frost break down rocks to make stones. Stones that have become smooth as they rub against each other are called pebbles.

Sand is often made of millions of tiny pieces of rock. Each piece is called a grain.

Sand feels soft when you touch it. Children play with it on the beach and in sandpits.

Rock keywords
Natural
Boulder
Pebble
Sand

Where do rocks come from?

It takes millions of years to make rock. There is a layer of rock right round the Earth. It is called the crust. There are many different kinds of rock.

Some rocks, such as pumice, came from **volcanoes**. Pumice is a very light rock. It is full of holes made by bubbles of air. We rub pumice stones on our body to keep skin smooth.

Another kind of rock was once under the sea. Chalk is very soft rock made from crushed seashells. It can be made into sticks and used for writing with.

Some rocks, such as marble, were once a boiling liquid, which cooled and became solid. This kind of rock is very hard. Marble can be polished to make it shine.

Rock keywords

Pumice
Chalk
Marble

Mining and quarrying

Rock is a very useful material because it is hard and strong. We get rock from **mines** and **quarries**.

Some rock is a long way underground so we have to dig to get it out. This is called mining.

When rock on the surface or in hillsides is cut away, it is called quarrying.

This rock in a quarry has been broken up by **explosives**. The bits of rock will be washed and sorted into different sizes.

Rock keywords
Mining
Quarrying
Explosives

The rock that comes from a quarry is called stone. Stone has to be cut using machines like this one.

Building materials

Rock is very strong and lasts for a long time. It is also waterproof. These things make it a good building material.

● Blocks of stone can be used for the walls of buildings. Builders use different types of stone for their colour and pattern.

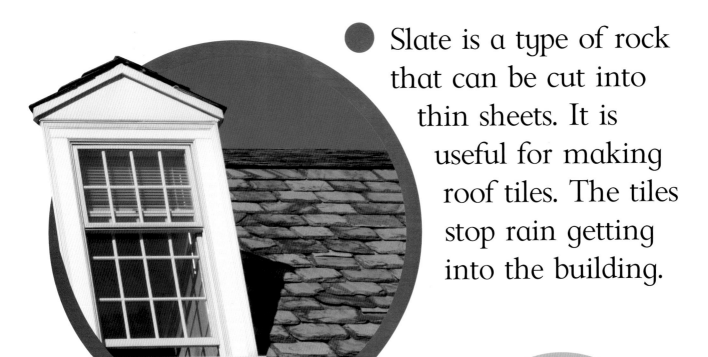

● Slate is a type of rock that can be cut into thin sheets. It is useful for making roof tiles. The tiles stop rain getting into the building.

● Tiny pieces of rock are called gravel. Gravel is usually found in rivers or on the sea bed. A **driveway** is sometimes covered with gravel.

Rock keywords

Strong
Waterproof
Gravel

Cement and concrete

Cement and **concrete** are strong building materials, which are made from rocks.

Cement is a mixture of crushed **limestone** rock and **clay**.

Builders mix cement with sand and water to make **mortar**. They use mortar to stick bricks together to make walls.

Concrete is an even stronger material made out of cement, sand, gravel and water. It is mixed in a concrete mixer like this one.

When the concrete is first mixed, it is a sticky paste. When it dries, it becomes very hard and strong.

We can make concrete objects in different shapes by pouring wet concrete into **moulds** and letting it dry.

Rock keywords
Cement
Limestone
Mortar
Concrete

Building with concrete

All buildings need a firm base on the ground underneath them so that they do not fall down. This base is called the **foundation**.

Foundations are made out of tough concrete.

Tall buildings are made of concrete because stone would be too heavy.

Concrete can be made even stronger by putting metal rods inside it. This is called **reinforced concrete**.

Rock keywords
Reinforced
Foundation
Polished

Concrete is grey and often rough. To make concrete buildings look nicer, thin sheets of coloured stone are sometimes glued to the outside. This building is covered in sheets of polished marble.

At home

Rocks and stones are nice to look at and some are very **hard-wearing**.

Some kitchens have **granite** worktops. Granite is a speckled rock. You can put hot pans on it and it will not burn. You can cut food on it and it will not get scratched.

This hard stone pestle (stick) and mortar (bowl) are used to grind food into powder.

Floor tiles are often made of stone. Stone stays cool and helps to keep houses cool in hot weather.

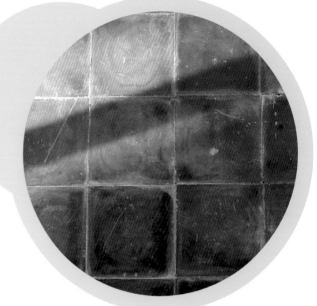

Stone is used for fireplaces because it does not burn.

Rock keywords
Cool
Beautiful
Hard-wearing
Granite

Marble is a beautiful rock. It is used for basins, floors, chopping boards and bowls.

In the street

Rocks and stones are very important for building roads because they are strong.

Roads need to be very hard-wearing so they can take the weight of heavy lorries without **crumbling**.

They are made using a layer of large stones, then a layer of smaller stones. This is covered by a smooth top layer of concrete or **asphalt**.

● Granite is a very hard stone. It is used to make the edges of pavements (kerbstones). It lasts for a long time.

● Pavements are usually made of **slabs** of concrete. The slabs are very cheap to make.

● *Rock keywords*

Pavement
Hard
Slab
Cheap

21

In the garden

Rocks and stones have a lot of different uses in the garden. We choose them because they are strong and waterproof, or just because they look nice.

Gravel is used to make garden paths.

Garden seats are sometimes made out of stone. They can be left outside in all types of weather.

Stone is used to make **containers** to grow plants in. Stone is heavy, so the containers do not get blown over by the wind.

Rocks and stones in art

Rock can be cut, shaped and polished. It is a good material for artists to work with.

An artist can use sharp tools to chip away at a block of stone to make a shape. This is called a sculpture.

An artist who does this is called a sculptor.

Marble is often used for making sculptures because it has beautiful patterns in it and it can be polished to make it shine.

Rock keywords
Cut
Shape
Polish
Mosaic

In **Roman times** artists often made **mosaic** floors out of small pieces of stone. They used different colours to make patterns and pictures of people and animals.

Gemstones

Inside some big rocks are precious stones called gemstones.

When gemstones are cut and polished, they sparkle, so they make beautiful jewellery, such as this ring.

Some gemstones are expensive because they are difficult to find.

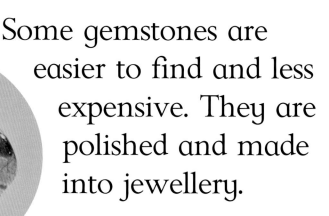

Some gemstones are easier to find and less expensive. They are polished and made into jewellery.

Diamonds are gemstones. They are hard and colourless. Large diamonds are made into jewellery.

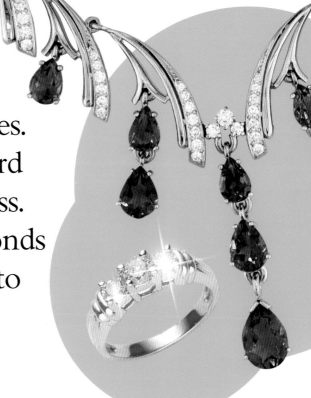

Small diamonds are used to cut with. They are fixed to the edge of knives and saws. The blade of this saw has tiny diamonds on it. It can cut through metal.

Rock keywords

Gemstone
Diamond

Glossary

Asphalt A substance made from oil, which is used as a surface on roads.

Cement A fine powder of limestone and clay. It is mixed with water and sand to make mortar; or with water, sand and small stones to make concrete.

Clay A type of fine earth which can be used to make bricks, ceramics and cement.

Concrete A mixture of cement, water, sand and small stones. It is used to build with.

Containers Objects, such as cartons, cans, jars, or boxes, used for holding or carrying things.

Crumbling Breaking up.

Diamonds Colourless gems. Diamond is the hardest rock there is.

Driveway A hard path for a car, which leads from the street to a house.

Explosives Substances used to blow up things into little bits, making a loud noise as they do so.

Foundation The base beneath a building.

Granite A very hard rock with a speckled pattern, which comes in different colours.

Hard-wearing To last a long time without breaking or rotting.

Limestone A white rock used to make cement.

Mines Holes dug in the ground to get rocks and minerals out.

Mortar A mixture of cement, sand and water that is used to stick bricks or stones together. It hardens when it is dry.

Mosaic A picture or design made from small coloured pieces of stone or tile fixed to a surface.

Moulds Containers in special shapes, into which liquids can be poured. When a liquid cools in a mould it becomes a solid in the shape of the mould.

Natural material Comes from the Earth, plants or animals.

Quarries Places where stone is dug from the ground.

Reinforced concrete Concrete made stronger by adding metal rods.

Roman times A time in history about 2,000 years ago, when the Romans, a people from Italy, ruled a large part of the world.

Slabs Thick pieces of something.

Volcanoes Openings in the Earth's crust through which very hot liquid rock called lava can flow.

Index

art 24, 25
asphalt 20, 28

boulders 6
bricks 14
building materials
  12, 13, 14, 15, 16, 17

cement 14, 15, 28
chalk 9
clay 14, 28
concrete 15, 16, 17,
  20, 21, 28
concrete mixers 15

diamonds 27, 28
driveways 13, 28

Earth's crust 8
explosives 11, 28

fireplaces 19
floor tiles 19
foundations 16, 28

gardens 22, 23
garden seats 23
gemstones 26, 27
granite 18, 21, 28

gravel 13, 15, 22

hard-wearing
  materials 18, 20,
  21, 29

jewellery 26, 27

kerbstones 21

lava 29
limestone 14, 29

machines 11
marble 9, 17, 19, 25
mines 10, 29
mining 10
mortar 14, 29
mosaic 25, 29
moulds 15, 29

natural materials
  6, 29

paths 22
pavements 21
pebbles 7
pestle and mortar
  18

plant containers
  23, 28
pumice 8

quarries 11, 29
quarrying 10

reinforced
  concrete 17, 29
roads 20
rock 6, 8
roof tiles 13

sand 7, 14, 15
sculpture 24, 25
sheets 13, 17
slabs 21, 29
slate 13
stone 11, 12, 18, 19,
  23, 25
stones 6, 7, 20

volcanoes 8, 29

waterproof
  material 12, 22
worktops 10